IN THE
NATIONAL INTEREST

General Sir John Monash once exhorted a graduating class to 'equip yourself for life, not solely for your own benefit but for the benefit of the whole community'. At the university established in his name, we repeat this statement to our own graduating classes, to acknowledge how important it is that common or public good flows from education.

Universities spread and build on the knowledge they acquire through scholarship in many ways, well beyond the transmission of this learning through education. It is a necessary part of a university's role to debate its findings, not only with other researchers and scholars, but also with the broader community in which it resides.

Publishing for the benefit of society is an important part of a university's commitment to free intellectual inquiry. A university provides civil space for such inquiry by its scholars, as well as for investigations by public intellectuals and expert practitioners.

This series, In the National Interest, embodies Monash University's mission to extend knowledge and encourage informed debate about matters of great significance to Australia's future.

Professor Susan Elliott AM
Interim President and Vice-Chancellor,
Monash University

LUCINDA HOLDFORTH

21ST-CENTURY VIRTUES: HOW THEY ARE FAILING OUR DEMOCRACY

MONASH
UNIVERSITY
PUBLISHING

Monash University Publishing
Matheson Library Annexe
40 Exhibition Walk
Monash University
Clayton, Victoria 3800, Australia
https://publishing.monash.edu

Monash University Publishing brings to the world publications which advance the best traditions of humane and enlightened thought.

ISBN: 9781922979094 (paperback)
ISBN: 9781922979117 (ebook)

Series: In the National Interest
Editor: Greg Bain
Project manager & copyeditor: Paul Smitz
Designer: Peter Long
Typesetter: Cannon Typesetting
Proofreader: John Mahony
Printed in Australia by Ligare Book Printers

A catalogue record for this book is available from the National Library of Australia.

The paper this book is printed on is in accordance with the standards of the Forest Stewardship Council®. The FSC® promotes environmentally responsible, socially beneficial and economically viable management of the world's forests.

21ST-CENTURY VIRTUES: HOW THEY ARE FAILING OUR DEMOCRACY

Personal virtues are back in fashion. In the twenty-first century, Australians are putting up their hands for moral thinking and right action. More than a few will openly scold those who fall short of their high standards. I'm also in favour of personal virtues. I think. I know I am nostalgic for a few vices. So the question arises: what exactly are the modern virtues?

Well, you only have to spend half an hour on LinkedIn—although I really don't recommend it—to note how the same concepts are elevated time and again: Authenticity, Empathy, Humility. A few others arise, generally along much the same lines. Self-Care is big. So is Vulnerability.

Yes, I suppose that Empathy, Humility and Vulnerability are nice. They are seemingly inoffensive.

The unkind might say they are insipid, as in fact I do. Is this the very best the 21st-century elite in Australia, as elsewhere, can offer by way of moral guidance to themselves and others? These modern virtues have something in common: they are self-referential. There's a relentless circling back to the individual's subjective state of being. Imagine an exercise in moral self-interrogation: am I authentically *me*? Am I looking after *moi* sufficiently well? Even though I'm so great, am I not also relatably *humble*?

Now consider this. The ancient Romans crowned themselves with laurels for Courage, Order and Vigour. These were the virtues of great conquerors and builders, social and economic planners, and their Roman virtues contributed materially to their long run of success.

China's vast hinterlands were once administered by a class of elite intellectuals who maintained order and hierarchy in an imperial system. The Confucian virtues of Ritual, Respect and Education were central to the longevity of the Chinese model.

The pre-Socratic Greeks prized Self-Knowledge, Proportion and, above all, Excellence—their term for excellence, *areté*, was synonymous with virtue. No wonder they produced not only astounding art, architecture and drama but also, arguably, the biggest intellectual innovations in history, including the invention of democracy itself.

The distinctive virtues prized by these civilisations shaped their cultures and underpinned their greatest achievements. And what qualities do we value in today's advanced democratic societies? It seems to me that we prize individual uniqueness, personal experiences of reality, and the quest for self-acceptance and self-love. These highly subjective measures of goodness are well represented on the world's number-one professional networking site, LinkedIn, the online town square for otherwise fact-driven, number-crunching achievers, many of whom hold or aspire to leadership roles across private and public sector domains.

The danger I see is that these self-involved qualities, when made the measure of mental and social health, inevitably undermine the task of building confident, engaged citizens. This matters because we need capable champions of democracy for the sake of our nation, and if we are to have any hope of forging a sustainable future for our broiling planet. Waiting to take advantage of this situation are disaffected right-wingers and cynics, all too happy to present themselves as serving up a larger vision of society than the petty narcissisms and intense subjectivity of the left. Meanwhile, the cult of the self becomes ideal fodder for the predations and profiteering of neoliberalism.

The larger political risk is that these forces come together in the form of a right-wing political messiah backed by unscrupulous business interests. Unlikely in Australia, of course, but by no means impossible. We no longer have the luxury of assuming that any democracy is inevitable or unbreakable. Donald Trump has shown us that anything can happen. Yet we maunder along, beset by the enervating principles of vulnerability and self-care. Self. Bloody. Care. How on earth are we going to preserve our democracy with self-care?

Of course, we may weakly console ourselves that the elevation of these self-referential qualities in theory does not automatically mean they are widely put into practice. Hypocrisy is a hallmark of our age, as of any age. We put the virtues we admire on a pedestal and much of the time we admire them from a safe distance, unless we are performing them loudly for public applause. But even mere lip service to ideals must count for something. Hypocrisy, as the canny French duke and moralist François de la Rochefoucauld said a long time ago, is the tribute that vice pays to virtue.[1] Even an insincere 'tribute' to a canon of virtues will influence the culture and shape the way society works.

So I ask myself: how did these modern virtues come to be so lauded? Who decided that these qualities *in particular* are the essence of good character in the twenty-first century, the century when everything is up for grabs, including our democracies, including our very planet?

NO MORE NAY-SAYING

I grew up in a Catholic world where virtue was mostly defined in the negative. The Ten Commandments consisted mostly of Thou-Shalt-Nots: no adultery, no stealing, no killing, no taking God's name in vain, no other god but this one, no graven images. And no, I hadn't the faintest idea what constituted a graven image. These commandments, handed down by God in his cloud to Moses on Mount Sinai, became a source of virtue-propagation for all the people of 'The Book': first the Jews, then the Christians, and later Muslims too. They were still being reinforced for us Catholics in suburban Sydney in the 1970s through parables, sermons, hymns and prayers. It was a brainwashing system designed to consolidate certain prohibitive ways of thinking in my young mind.

While I understood that Catholics were not among the elite—through most of the twentieth century to that point, Protestants had clearly dominated Australian politics and business—nevertheless I felt we were part of a broad rational stream of Australian life. Now, when I look back on the rituals I was required to undergo as a child, such as trembling with unknowing guilt at confession, kneeling in homage to the broken Jesus on his crucifix, and copping bizarre lectures about saints and the Virgin and the Devil, it feels as though I was brought up in a mad cult.

I still shake my head at the things we were required to believe, do and say. And that doesn't include the revelations of recent years about the institutional abuse of children and Church cover-ups.

Protestantism probably preserved Christianity in Western culture long after the latter's expiration date. With an emphasis on individual effort and delayed gratification, Protestant virtues propelled and upheld the rising middle class, the capitalist system and the making of our modern world. Long after Christianity had lost any rational authority, the definition of a virtuous life in Western culture could still be summed up in a few dismal words: if it looks like fun, *don't do it*.

This self-denying morality system was perhaps most completely embodied, in the public imagination at least, by the late British monarch Queen Elizabeth II. Historian William Dalrymple said as much on the day of her death in September 2022:

> I never expected to be so moved, or so shaken, by the death of the Queen … Whatever your views on the monarchy, it was a life that represented virtues valued by a generation that has now passed, and whose absence daily diminishes public life: duty, service, stoicism, humility, decency, commitment, constancy and stability. RIP.[2]

As thousands of people queued up over days to farewell the encoffined Queen, I had the distinct impression that the modern world was farewelling the monarch's self-denying virtues along with her person. Sad to see them go but resigned to their passing. Perhaps what is most remarkable is that it took us so long to wave those virtues goodbye.

After all, it was way back in 1882 that self-proclaimed *immoralist* Friedrich Nietzsche announced that God was dead. This disillusioned descendant of a line of gloomy German Lutheran pastors knew very well the implications of this revelation. If God was dead, then his biblical commandments were evidently defunct. To convince everyone else of the need for a new paradigm, Nietzsche set about mocking and undermining the entire Christian mindset, with its prohibitive spirit and its antipathy to the human body and sensual pleasures. If God is dead, he asked, then why are we still obeying these dreary, life-denying Christian rules? Why are we behaving like a herd of obedient domesticated animals? Why aren't we thinking for ourselves?

A classicist himself, Nietzsche drew inspiration from the vibrant pagan worlds of classical Greece and Rome. He was especially enamoured of the aristocratic mindset of ancient Greece in the period before Socrates introduced philosophical doubt and scepticism. Here was an intensely creative environment where achievement was applauded, the will to power was healthy, and competition in every field of endeavour was celebrated. In *The Gay Science*, Nietzsche asked each of us to imagine living a life so richly intense in meaning and fulfilment that we would be ready to live it all over again. The goal was amor fati: to love one's own fate. The life to which he himself aspired was not some austere nineteenth-century existence based on Christian bourgeois rules, picking apart the failings of oneself or others, but one of affirmation and beauty:

> I want to learn more and more to see as beautiful what is necessary in things; then I shall be one of those who make things beautiful. Amor fati: let that be my love henceforth! I do not want to wage war against what is ugly. I do not want to accuse; I do not even want to accuse those who accuse. *Looking away* shall be my only negation. And all in all and on the whole: someday I wish to be only a Yes-sayer.[3]

When I was growing up, without knowing a thing about Nietzsche, I too wanted to be a yes-sayer. I said yes to any number of vices, especially the vices that Catholics fondly referred to as those 'little sins of the body'. As for the virtues, I had little interest in my own or anyone else's. Instead of morality, I had causes. I marched for Aboriginal land rights, for International Women's Day, against US nuclear bases in Australia. I went to fundraisers against apartheid.

I generally judged people this way: if you voted Labor you were probably OK, as long as you were in favour of equality—for women, Indigenous Australians, disabled people, migrants, gay men and women, everyone. The agenda I advocated was very pragmatic, or so I felt, around amending laws and regulations.

Since then, Australia has indeed eliminated or amended numerous bad laws that served to discriminate negatively. Yet true inclusion has still to be achieved. So there is an unfinished agenda: to *make room*. Hence, women of all generations marching down the streets of Australian capital cities demanding change. Indigenous Australians calling for a Voice to Parliament. People living with disability pushing for full participation in our society. But while greater fairness, equality and inclusion will undoubtedly contribute to a more dynamic and successful democracy, we can't forget that democracy itself is the sine qua non of that progress. That's why the democratic centre must hold, and we can't simply assume it will. Our first yes must be to democracy.

THE REVALUATION OF VALUES

A while back, I went to stay at a friend's holiday house on the mid North Coast of New South Wales. As I walked into the children's room to put my bag on the bed, my eye was attracted by a simple frame on the wall containing chequered squares of faded rose and lemon yellow, some with images and words. It was an eighty-year-old snakes and ladders board. That's the game where you roll the dice and move your counter up from the bottom left-hand corner of the board, the winner being whoever lands first on the 100th square at the top right-hand corner. Land on the base of a ladder and your way upwards is accelerated, but hit upon a snake's hissing head and you are sent spiralling back down.

That snakes and ladders board, dating perhaps to the 1930s, was a lovely object in itself. It also offered a vivid snapshot of twentieth-century values, or more specifically the values of the Christian middle-class world. Looking at this board, you could easily imagine that Nietzsche had never happened.

The square at the base of each ladder portrayed the name of a human virtue: Self-Denial, Faith, Pity, Kindness, Truthfulness, Forgiveness, Obedience and Penitence. The accompanying images ranged from a gentleman giving alms to an old lady (Pity), to a seated woman with a scarved head being looked at regretfully by a man (Self-Denial), to a man on his knees in prayer (Penitence) and a resigned boy-soldier accepting his death in a circle of fire on a ship's deck (Obedience). All very Queen Elizabeth II. Unbelievably un-Nietzschean.

If you landed on the head of a snake, on the other hand, you had hit on a vice. Consistent with a nay-saying Christian culture, there were many more vices than virtues. Avarice was apparently the worst crime of all: if you landed on that gigantic snake's head near the top of the board, you slithered almost the whole way back to the start. After Avarice came, presumably in descending order of sinfulness, Pride, Selfishness, Anger, Slander, Depravity, Cruelty, Quarrelsomeness, Dishonesty, Frivolity, Vanity, Covetousness and Unpunctuality. Good behaviour took you up to Heaven; bad behaviour hurtled you down to board-game Hell. A rich field for anyone fascinated by changes in social mores, as I'm sure you'll agree.

I must admit that I became unduly fixated on Unpunctuality as a vice. For a moment I was almost weepy with nostalgia for a world in which being late was a sin. I sometimes feel like one of the last poor sad saps in modern life who is not only compulsively punctual but compulsively *pre-punctual*. Which means I usually receive a text at the agreed time that says, 'Hi! I haven't forgotten and I'm leaving home now.' So, that'll be half an hour more waiting then. And I can't complain because Unpunctuality is no longer a vice.

Among the other lost vices, Avarice today is simple common sense in our insecure economic jungle, and Vanity is psychologically healthy self-care. Covetousness is essential to neoliberalism: it is why we can be beguiled by the advertising industry to experience the economically useful pleasure of desire. The vice of Pride on the board appeared as a pompous chap with a top hat and a lifted chin, waving his cane. Today, personal pride is generally encouraged, except for people who've had any worldly success, who are now required to be *humble*.

Penitence is an interesting one. I think it has largely disappeared, except in a few painfully honest domains like Alcoholics Anonymous, where you are asked to acknowledge the harm you've done to others and where possible make amends. But we do hear a lot about Shame, which used to be a noun, meaning a personal response to one's own moral failure. Now it is a verb, meaning a cruel attempt to make someone else feel bad for no good reason. See: slut-shame, victim-shame, body-shame. The perverse result is that genuine personal shame and penitence are almost non-existent. It is true that Penitence is routinely performed by our politicians and senior business leaders, but only once they are caught out.

Then there is Frivolity, which falls into a different category of erasure. It was depicted on the snakes and ladders board by two happy girls capering in flapper dresses. They looked so charming that I assumed Frivolity was classified as a virtue. How nice, I thought, before realising my mistake. Frivolity as a vice relied upon the threat that shameless cavorting posed to the solemn traditions and rituals of bourgeois life. But today almost no occasion is sacred. Weddings are more like three-day music festivals. Even modern funerals have been reclassified from sombre mourning rituals to 'life celebrations'. If Frivolity is no longer a vice, can 'frivolity' be committed at all? And you would really have to make an effort these days if you wanted to plead guilty to Depravity.

But the virtues too are under siege. Obedience: is that still a virtue? To obey unquestioningly is to make yourself subservient to others, an intolerable idea in this age of autonomy. How about Anger? It is seen as a positive attribute, allied to self-expression, although in its modern incarnation it routinely sits side by side with outcries of personal grievance and self-pity. Anger as a healthful outlet for personal pain. And in this age of intolerance, Forgiveness, possibly the most beautiful of the virtues, is in very short supply.

It could be said, of course, that we moderns rarely think consciously in terms of 'vices' or 'sins' at all. Bad behaviour is routinely contextualised, personalised and pathologised. Even crimes and evil acts are quite often treated as symptoms of an individual's unique circumstances or the expression of an ongoing personal problem. It could be depression or bipolarity or ADHD or anxiety or autism or addiction or work stress or discrimination or economic or social disadvantage. The list keeps growing.

Slander, Cruelty and Dishonesty are still hateful acts to a modern mind. But it is amazing how often public figures, when caught red-handed and forced to admit to some vile deed, will quickly make a pro-forma apology, then revert to extenuating circumstances that warrant not only our fair consideration but even our sympathy. Footballers, politicians, CEOs and movie stars are masters of the art of converting their misdeeds into heartfelt pleas and moving cries for understanding, love and acceptance. And yes, even forgiveness. Because, after all, they are vulnerable too.

BRENÉ BROWN AND THE NEW COMMANDMENTS

Our 21st-century virtues have come down to us not from the celestial cloud but via its modern high-tech equivalent. I date their arrival to a June day in 2010 when an insightful, self-deprecating and charming American woman named Brené Brown gave a TED talk in Houston that is still one of the most watched ever. It was called 'The Power of Vulnerability'.

Brown said that 'Connection, the ability to feel connected, is how we are wired, is why we are here'. Despite its manifest importance, however, her research showed there was a severe lack of human connection in our modern societies. This deficit, she argued, was caused by our feelings of shame and fear, and the struggle for a sense of worthiness. The result? Brown said memorably of present-day America that it had the most in-debt, obese, addicted and medicated adult cohort in US history. She pointed to the broader social ramifications of these sad trends: the more that people were afraid and uncertain, the more they turned to dogma, polarisation and blame to discharge their pain and discomfort. My take on her words? Lonely, ashamed, angry people pose a threat to strong civic and democratic community life.[4]

Those who achieved a feeling of connection, on the other hand, said Brown, had the courage to tell the story of who they were with their whole heart. They were brave enough to be imperfect, compassionate enough to be kind to themselves first and then to reach out to others. They let go of who they thought they should be, in order to be who they really were. They embraced vulnerability, and they believed that what made them vulnerable made them beautiful. Her point was this: if we all practised openly being our authentic, vulnerable selves, we might find more fulfilling connections with other people and lead better lives.

A dozen years on from that speech, there is an entire universe of Brené Brown: Brené Brown books, Brené Brown films, Brené Brown podcasts.

Vulnerability was just the beginning of Brené Brown's program to make us happier and more wholehearted people.

I have three of Brown's books. One is called *Daring Greatly: How the Courage to Be Vulnerable Transforms the Way We Live, Love, Parent and Lead*.[5] It's a perfect title, designed to include absolutely everyone in her generous, heartfelt world. Inside the cover, Brown explains the source of her title. 'Daring greatly' is a quote from a famous speech by US president Theodore Roosevelt in which he excoriates the critics on the sidelines for their sniping, easy takedowns of those who participate in public life. The Roosevelt speech celebrates 'the man in the arena', the one who takes the risks, who sometimes fails, who knows 'great enthusiasms, the great devotions; who spends himself in a worthy cause'.[6]

Teddy Roosevelt was famous for his own causes: a 'trust-busting' battle against American monopoly businesses, outrageously invading both the Philippines and Cuba, and fighting off miners and developers to sequester some of America's greatest wildernesses into national parks. But what is the worthy cause that Brené Brown's *Daring Greatly* is devoted to? What is the great dare she addresses? She says it is about the courage to be vulnerable: 'We must dare to show up and be seen.' That's it. That's daring greatly. Bathos at its best.

Another book is called *Dare to Lead*.[7] According to the subtitle, it's about 'Daring Greatly and Rising Strong at Work'. Yes, I'm mystified by that 'Rising Strong' bit too. It has a slightly erectile quality, doesn't it, perhaps ideally suited to the business audiences it is aimed at. Apparently, this book emerged from work that Brown did with 'leadership groups all around the world'. The back cover has enthusiastic recommendations from Sheryl Sandberg, then COO of Facebook, and Ed Catmull, at that time president of the Pixar and Disney Animation studios.

The third Brown book I own is called *The Gifts of Imperfection: Let Go of Who You Think You're Supposed to Be and Embrace Who You Are*.[8] The preface says: 'Owning our story and loving ourselves through that process is the bravest thing that we will ever do.' Speaking for myself, I sincerely hope not. A few pages in, Brown offers this prayer: 'May we find the courage to let go of who we think we're supposed to be so that we can fully embrace our authentic selves—the imperfect, the creative, the vulnerable, the powerful, the broken, and the beautiful.' I had to stop reading the book right there.

And now I am reminded of the strong impression made upon me on 6 January 2021, as I watched footage of that horde invading the US Capitol. I did not see lonely, isolated, depressed people lacking the courage to embrace their authentic selves. I saw an exuberant and energised anti-democratic mob.

AUTHENTICITY: THE META-VIRTUE

After my encounter with the morality board game at the house by the sea, I wondered if our new values of Authenticity, Vulnerability and Empathy represented a belated response to Nietzsche's spirited call, an attempt to live by life-affirming humanist values in a world without God or Devil, Heaven or Hell, a world where life is worth living and rich in meaning for its own sake. Now it seems to me that Authenticity may be the modern meta-virtue.

To say that something is authentic is to validate a deeply fundamental and worthwhile idea: this painting or product is what it says it is. Genuine. The real deal. And the real thing has infinitely more value than any fake or even a worshipful copy. Authenticity in a human being is surely what makes us reliable and trustworthy. What could possibly be more important? But I am cautious here because let us recall, putting aside the pages of Brené Brown's books, that it is on LinkedIn, that entirely dubious source of human wisdom, where authentic leadership is most loudly proclaimed as the wave of the future. Well, there, but also at the Harvard Business School executive education program.[9]

I note that authenticity was never the leadership wave of the pre-LinkedIn past. For most of human history, any leader whose primary focus was on retaining this virtue was, in retrospect at least, considered to be self-indulgent, if not downright dangerous. Like King Charles 1, who was so attached to his own Catholicism and the principle of autocratic sovereignty that he refused to compromise with his parliament, thereby setting England on the path to a traumatic civil war. Charles was so stubbornly devoted to virtue that he lost his own head in defence of it. Other leaders have sacrificed their own 'authentic' principles to achieve what they saw as the greater good. Henry IV of France reluctantly converted to Catholicism to unite his divided country and thereby set France on the path to glory. 'Paris is worth a Mass,' Henry IV famously said, and it undoubtedly was.

Franklin D Roosevelt is considered one of the great US presidents. He was no racist, but to secure the support of Southern Democrats for his New Deal, he knowingly discriminated against Black Americans in the design of numerous Depression-busting programs. He did this to get those measures passed through Congress for what he perceived as the overall good of the American people in a time of desperate economic need. If you think that was a dodgy compromise, consider this: some people reckon FDR consciously sacrificed Pearl Harbor in

December 1941 to get America into World War II and save global democracy.

Here's another example. In 2008, as the American financial system was at risk of collapse, another progressive Democrat, presidential candidate Barack Obama, decided to back an enormous bank bailout bill to prop up the thieves and knaves of Wall Street rather than let the US and global economies fall apart. Here was a man who was not the least bit interested in looking out for billionaires. But he ruptured his own belief system when he deemed that circumstances demanded it. I suspect he regrets that one but would probably still argue today that he had no choice.

Time and again, good leaders have acted against their own principles for what they regarded as the greater good. They've chosen to corrupt their own souls rather than weaken the body politic. They've had to deny or even overcome their authentic selves. If they had put their personal authenticity first, would they have lived more meaningful lives? More importantly, would they have been better leaders?

I have tried to recall instances of Australian prime ministers wrestling mightily with their consciences. Luckily for us, our leaders have tended not to be unduly burdened by conscience and therefore stayed open to pragmatic compromise. A notable exception was John Curtin, who was a deeply moral individual and a genuine pacifist. He found himself obliged by the national interest to lead Australians into the bloodbath of World War II. He did exactly the right thing, but it must have hurt him deeply. He died before peace was finally achieved.

While self-knowledge was a profoundly important Greek virtue—'Know Yourself' was one of the three injunctions in the forecourt of the Temple of Delphi—authenticity in our modern sense was not. Man is a political animal, Aristotle pointed out in about 350 BCE. It is in our nature to live together, like bees in a hive, within a polis or organised community. That means we are by no means self-sufficient individuals. We are of no use to ourselves or anyone else if we cultivate our virtues in splendid isolation. The well-being of the group is a necessary precondition to all and any individual needs, ethics and choices. Given Aristotle's world view, we should not be surprised that he doesn't say a word about behaving 'authentically'. He thought the aim was to strike the 'golden mean', responding to our circumstances 'at the right times, about the right things, towards the right people, for the right end, and in the right way'. This, he said in his *Nicomachean Ethics*, 'is proper to virtue'.

Don't we all play roles throughout our lives? Don't we adjust our manner and our demeanour to fit with our lovers, our bosses, our friends, our grandparents, our neighbours, even the customer service person at the other end of a long wait on the phone?

To live in a community is to fit the self to circumstance, to offer the self that best matches the moment. We are all far more than one true thing. We are, I think, many true things jostling and colliding and jangling against each other. And the adaptations we make are by no means necessarily diminutions of authentic selfhood. As we respond to other people and circumstances, as we discover more about ourselves, is it not the case that we grow and flourish, like flowers turning their faces to the changing movements of the sun?

In 2007 I wrote a short book about manners arguing that, despite their reputation as redundant conservators of old-fashioned privilege, these basic codes of behaviour were a simple way that we, as individuals in democracies, could respectfully encounter other individuals in the shared civic space.[10] Manners are, of course, fundamentally inauthentic. That is in fact their merit. They do not ask us to make the preservation of our own sacred authenticity the final standard of our social behaviour. On the contrary, we make these small concessions to preserve the dignity and integrity of very different individuals and to promote the smooth functioning of our communities.

Aristotle thought the aim of a virtue-filled life was not to cultivate some authentic purity, but to achieve eudemonia or 'human flourishing'. He described a person with 'greatness of soul' as one who believed himself to be worthy of great things, was in fact worthy of them, and managed to achieve those good things in the public sphere. As a result of his successful efforts, any 'great-souled man' was bound to be proud, self-satisfied and—how paradoxical this appears to the modern mind—indifferent to public opinion. Not necessarily, not even probably, a likeable person in the modern sense. Today, of course, a term of admiration for many leaders is that they are 'relatable'. I presume this means they remind us of our ordinary, authentic, approval-seeking selves. But do we really want to live in a democratic world so small-minded that our primary need of our leaders is that they be just like us? I for one do not.

Every life is one of change. If we resist the idea of human complexity, malleability and evolution, it leads, I think, to a dangerous kind of hardening and narrowing of perceptions of ourselves and each other. In 1984, when Saul Bellow was nearly seventy years old and had already won the Nobel Prize in Literature for novels that interrogated the modern human condition, he said to *The New York Times* hopefully: 'I am certain that there are human qualities still to be discovered.' He added: 'What is the unconscious after all? The unconscious is anything human beings don't know.'[11]

The glory of life in a democracy is precisely that we can permit ourselves to change and discover new facets of ourselves. Nietzsche wrote in some wonder of America that it was where 'the individual is convinced that he can do almost anything, that he can play almost any role, whereby everyone makes experiments with himself, improvises, tries anew, tries with delight, whereby all nature ceases and becomes art'.[12] And would it not be dangerous if people in charge felt they could not amend or over-turn their prior opinions, or concede some reasonable point to the opposing side, for fear of being accused of 'inauthenticity'?

The cold truth is that when people in high posi-tions think and talk about authenticity these days, they are often referring to their 'personal brand'. It's a repellent concept, but a powerful and lucrative one. Many people in the public eye—not only politicians but business leaders, athletes and celebrities too—will spend a great deal of time bolstering their authenticity credentials and avoiding any actions or statements that might conflict with their professional public image. No matter what they might really think. Even if they have changed their mind or are grappling with a mental or moral caveat to a former certainty. What a horrible trap.

And if none of this persuades you, remember this: the most awful people you know are probably entirely authentic.

VULNERABILITY IS OUR 'STRENGTH'

If Brené Brown wanted us to focus on our inner fragility, she should be well pleased. We are quivering like never before. The stiff upper lip has been replaced by a trembling lower one. We are vulnerable. We're easily hurt, we feel offended, we take offence, we accuse each other of gaslighting, we're thin-skinned, we're triggered, we're quitting, we're litigating, we're going home. We just can't take it anymore. Vulnerability is paradoxically nurtured by school systems devoted to ensuring children are no longer allowed to fail in any arena, with the possible exception of sport. The decline of objective merit as an academic standard inclines some children to withdraw from competition altogether and permits others to develop an irrational self-belief in their abilities.

In fact, in early life, children are well aware that some of them are better than others at certain tasks. So they're not particularly grateful for the phony boosterism. A ten-year-old of my acquaintance said recently that she *hates* those games where nobody wins. An eight-year-old I know likes to tell me about this amazing kid in their school who is the eleventh-fastest 400-metre runner in her age group in the state. Kids understand winning and losing. They respect it. Then they are asked to spend twelve years in a school system that downgrades the significance of any academic competition at all—until it comes to the secondary school certificate, when they are abruptly told that their entire future is on the line. Guess what? They have a nervous breakdown.

If there is one thing we humans really need to learn, it's how to fail without falling apart. Instead, we are now entitled to think of our vulnerable selves as more enlightened, not in spite of our increased fragility, but precisely because we are so aware of it. Our antennae are on the alert for incoming injuries. Anguished outrage is not an uncommon personal response to any perceived offence.

The elevation of Vulnerability as a virtue creates an environment increasingly antithetical to free speech. If my ideas are even remotely likely to offend your feelings, and you make it clear that experiencing bad feelings will put you 'at risk' or make you feel 'unsafe', then there is enormous pressure on me not to express my views. And thus we silence the vigorous exchange of views so essential to any democratic system.

We are all going to suffer, and we will all die, and yes, we will all fail at something that matters to us. So it's true, we are indeed vulnerable. That is the human condition. We are just Shakespeare's 'poor, bare, fork'd animals'. Vulnerable to loss and pain; to insults, threats and slights; to indifference, exclusion and underestimation. Prone to our own delusions, dreams and fears, our traumatic memories and improbable fantasies. Susceptible to disease and death, accident and misadventure. Doomed to disappointment and disillusion. And, absolutely, some of us are more vulnerable than others to active or passive discrimination on the grounds of our race, appearance, age, gender, sexual orientation, body shape, injuries, disabilities, and sometimes even our abilities.

But does any of this make vulnerability a virtue? Should it? Wouldn't that be rather like turning, say, the human condition of being prone to hay fever into a virtue? Or put it this way: is vulnerability something we should actively aspire to? The etymology of 'vulnerability' is directly linked to the Latin 'vulnus' meaning 'wound'. What does an overactive focus on our own capacity to be hurt do for us as individuals or the communities in which we live?

Is dwelling on vulnerability, especially by people with comfortable middle-class lives, positive? Or is it dangerously self-indulgent and, ultimately and ironically, self-fulfilling? Perhaps this explains the current fashion for cultivating greater 'resilience'. It seems we have designed a virtue so culturally corrosive that it acts like a disease and requires a cure.

Fortunately, we have some vivid counter-examples to stiffen our wobbling spines. Like Greta Thunberg, the Swedish climate activist who, at a Youth 4 Climate Summit in Milan in 2021, stood up and mocked politicians around the world for their climate change platitudes. 'Build back better blah blah blah,' she said. 'Green economy blah blah blah. Net zero by 2050 blah blah blah.' An iconic figure with her stern face, her uncompromising words, her moral authority. People say her autism helps her, lends her courage. I suspect that is meant to let the rest of us off the hook. It should not.

Or Penny Wong, the Australian Foreign Minister. She's cool, she's deliberative and dagger-sharp. When she speaks to us in that calm low voice, we lean forward to hear her words. As a minister, Wong has spoken publicly of the racism she's faced in Australia. She has done so as a leader acknowledging a reality in our society that we need to deal with, aware that her example and experience can help others. It's not a show of vulnerability but a demonstration of her strength.

As New Zealand's prime minister, Jacinda Ardern was warm and natural while opinionated and decisive. When she resigned in January 2023, before an upcoming election, articles were written about the unique pressure women leaders are under, the understandable need she must have felt for self-care, the strains and stresses Jacinda bravely bore but which in the end broke her. In fact, she is a canny politician: her polling was bad, she saw the light and she headed for the exit. Good on her. She's already embarking on an international career. Let's not automatically attribute frailty to a realistic woman in charge of her destiny.

We all have our weaknesses, but we surely need not hunt for vulnerability where it doesn't need to exist. Let's not talk it up. Let's refuse to sell it as an ideal to young women or young men, as some essential, meritorious part of a good and worthy life.

TRANSPARENCY OUTRANKS PRIVACY

Authentic people are up-front, aren't they? Nothing to hide. Always ready to disclose the situation when asked, or better still, even before they are asked: the truth, the whole truth, and nothing but the truth. So in the modern virtue system, where authenticity is the meta-virtue, Transparency is necessarily an unmitigated good. A guard against bad people—especially bad leaders—with shady pasts and murky motives, a protection against hypocrisy and humbug. We routinely hear leaders use their personal experiences to explain and justify their policies and decisions. Personal transparency, even more than a piece of objectively well-founded, fair-minded policy reasoning, gives rise to confidence and trust.

In this digital and therapeutic era, we should not be astonished at just how much of their private lives modern people are willing to disclose. To anyone. To everyone. Especially for money, but often for free.

The veil between the home and the world has now been lifted. Famous and unfamous people show themselves getting dressed. Putting on their make-up. Admiring themselves in the bathroom mirror. Squeezing their pimples. Lying in bed. Naked. Having sex. Fighting, crying, ranting. Public and private lives, once separate, are now conjoined. This oversharing trend may sometimes be seen as mildly irritating or laughed off as a bore. But old-fashioned reticence? Now *that* is just plain underhanded, sneaky, suspicious.

The mania for self-explanation and self-exposure means that the concept of a valuable private life is almost meaningless today. At no small cost. 'A life spent entirely in public, in the presence of others, becomes ... shallow,' wrote political theorist Hannah Arendt.[13] I think of this quote every time I see one of those highly choreographed clips of a 'random act of kindness' on social media. An odious young man films himself as he 'spontaneously' pushes an overblown bunch of flowers into the reluctant hands of an older woman who is sitting in a food hall in her comfortable dress, having a coffee and minding her own business. Dragging her unwillingly into the public spotlight for the sake of his own ego.

We may marvel at the emptiness of so much modern living, but there are broader political implications to be considered. George Orwell addressed this question in his 1941 essay 'England Your England'. This is an unsentimental love letter to his country and its civilisation as it faces the prospect of being wiped out by the Nazi war machine. It begins with the arresting line: 'As I write, highly civilized human beings are flying overhead, trying to kill me.'[14]

Orwell writes about an English characteristic that is 'so much a part of us that we barely notice it'. It is, he says, 'the addiction to hobbies and spare time occupations, the privateness of English life. We are a nation of flower lovers but also a nation of stamp-collectors, pigeon-fanciers, amateur carpenters, coupon-snippers, darts-players, crossword-puzzle fans.' Orwell reminds the reader that British culture that is most truly 'native' centres around 'things which even when they are communal are not official—the pub, the football match, the back garden, the fireside inn, and the "nice cup of tea".' Orwell explicitly connects this English attachment to private, unofficial and unaffiliated pleasures to the idea of liberal democracy itself:

The liberty of the individual is still believed in … the liberty to have a home of your own, to do what you like in your spare time, to choose your own amusements instead of having them chosen for you from above. The most hateful of all names in an English ear is Nosey Parker.

Authoritarian regimes are renowned for being Nosey Parkers. The unification of private and public life, the erasure of the distinction between them, is a hallmark of totalitarianism in any of its forms. Most modern tyrannies are nation-sized criminal enterprises, a system they protect by keeping their populations to greater or lesser extents isolated, information-deprived and under surveillance.

The novelist Milan Kundera knows this only too well, having experienced the 1968 Soviet invasion of his country, Czechoslovakia, when the Russians took control of all aspects of citizens' lives. Kundera saw and defended the singular importance of what he called modern man's 'intimate life'. It was, he said, 'one's personal secret, something valuable, inviolable, the basis of one's originality'. What's more, he believed there should always be a division between private and public life:

> Only a hypocrite would say that such a border doesn't exist and that a man ought to be the same person in his public and intimate life. Any man who was the same in both public and intimate life would be a monster. He would be without spontaneity in his private life and without responsibility in his public life.[15]

In our time, the Murdoch press, that modern supporter of right-wing politicians, has shown us the evil that happens when private lives are unwillingly aired in public. For years, the *News of the World* newspaper illegally tapped the phones of its famous targets, outing their little secrets and in some cases all but destroying people's lives. Kundera described the totalitarian ideal as one where everyone lives in harmony, united by a common will and faith, 'without secrets from one another'.[16] *News of the World* is now gone, but the Murdoch machine rolls on.

In his 1941 essay, Orwell made this observation about the political importance of the private life:

> Like all other modern people, the English are in process of being numbered, labelled, conscripted, 'coordinated'. But the pull of their impulses is in the other direction and the kind of regimentation that can be imposed on them will be modified in consequence. No party rallies, no youth movements, no coloured shirts, no Jew-baiting or spontaneous demonstrations. No Gestapo either in all probability.

Orwell believed that the English love of the private life would be a protection against totalitarianism. Would he not be shocked at how many of us voluntarily relinquish that privacy, splashing details of our intimate selves and lives on TV, TikTok, OnlyFans, Facebook, Instagram and more?

Even the courtesy of protecting *other* people's privacy has disappeared. The other day, my Uber driver put his girlfriend on speakerphone and engaged with her in what was obviously an ongoing conversation about the flaws in their relationship. More specifically, the flaws in her. He spoke with cold disapproval; she was breathy and apologetic. He did not disclose to her that a stranger was sitting in the back seat, listening to every biting sentence from him and every nervous pause and sigh from her. There I sat, fascinated, ashamed and appalled.

How can we fight off the advances of media intrusion and the growth of a surveillance state if we give ourselves away, and others too, so freely, so fully, so frivolously? What will any of us have left with which to protect our intimate relationships, to preserve our own souls?

NEOLIBERALISM RIDES THE WAVE

In 2016, George Monbiot, writing in *The Guardian*, pointed to the same maladies Brené Brown high-lighted in 2010. Monbiot too deplored the 'epidemics of self-hate, eating disorders, depression, loneliness, performance anxiety and social phobia in our developed world'. Unlike Brown, however, Monbiot did not attribute this widespread misery to 'lack of connection' or our unwillingness to be 'vulnerable' in the presence of others. He said this poor state of affairs was caused by the rise of neoliberalism. 'Neoliberalism,' Monbiot said, works by 'redefining its citizens as consumers.' It is a world that revolves around the interests of the wealthy elite, with tax and regulation minimised, collective bargaining by labour limited or eliminated, and corporate power concentrated. It is a system where, as Monbiot says, 'business takes the profits, the state keeps the risk'.[17]

Well, we all know what neoliberalism feels like because we are living in it. This is the eradication of Aristotle's polis. Engaged and equal citizens are replaced in this dystopia by anxious, insecure gig-economy workers and passive consumers. Wealth and power are controlled by an unelected elite, resulting in the decline and decay of the public commons, the public spaces, the public utilities, the public good. Valued communal interests are progressively shut down, while isolated individuals make perfect targets for economic exploitation and ideal subjects for tyrannically minded politicians.

Monbiot's analysis cannot be dismissed as some resentful left-wing take on an inevitable modernity. Martin Wolf is the chief financial commentator for the *Financial Times*, respected by chairs and CEOs around the world. In his new book *The Crisis of Democratic Capitalism*, Wolf makes Monbiot's dark portrait of our present and future look rather optimistic. Wolf says bluntly that 'the insecurity laissez-faire capitalism generates for the great majority … is ultimately incompatible with democracy'.[18]

I worked in and with large Australian corporates for many years, and I saw even second-tier executives end up with more money than they knew what to do with. These executives rode on the history of a strong brand, sometimes a former government-created and owned brand, and watched their business thrive on a legacy of product recognition and community goodwill, plus a share-price boom on the stock market. Some executives I worked with were more talented than others, but most of them you wouldn't vote for on the strata committee of your apartment block, let alone elect to the local council. Their rise to outsize prosperity has been a major contributor to modern income inequality, along with the determined suppression of workers' real wages. The Australia Institute estimates that the top-earning 10 per cent of our country got 93 per cent of the benefits of economic growth in Australia between 2009 and 2019.[19]

An unusually honest retiring CEO—he'd become a multi-*multi*-millionaire—once told me that he could hardly believe he was ending his career with *so much money*. He would now have a full-time job managing his own vast personal wealth. Naturally, he gives more money to charity than you or I and is widely praised for it.

So here's my question: if the steamroller of neo-liberalism is the problem, how on earth will a focus on personal authenticity and vulnerability provide the solution?

CORPORATIONS WITH 'PURPOSE'

One of the most successful Brené Brown admirers is Australian 'mindset coach' Ben Crowe. Let us leave aside for the moment what it may tell us about our times that such a role can even exist. Crowe is best known for his most famous client, the universally adored tennis star Ash Barty, who won the French Open, Wimbledon and the Australian Open before quitting, aged twenty-six, at the top of her game. As part of an expansive newspaper profile by Melissa Fyfe in 2022, Crowe spoke about helping 'high performing' individuals like Barty and also the unnamed leaders of many organisations. His goal was not, he said, to help them achieve some external measure of success. He was not there to aid them in pursuit of the ambitions 'imposed' upon them by the outside world. No. It was all about helping them 'own their own story' and pursue their own dreams, presumably with professional success as a happy by-product. According to the article:

> Ben Crowe is asking Australians to be more vulnerable, kind and connected. To love ourselves unconditionally, cut ourselves some slack, and

unshackle from expectation and shame. He wants us to identify what's within our control and stop fighting what's outside it. Find purpose and serve others.[20]

Note how 'purpose' floats freely, untethered to any social goal, uninformed by any ethical framework. The phrase 'for purpose' was originally coined by not-for-profit agencies to clearly distinguish themselves from for-profit corporations. If you worked 'for purpose', you were committed to social good. Today, listed companies whose entire raison d'être is money-making will boast that they too have 'purpose'. Who cares what that purpose is?

Ash Barty credited Ben Crowe with giving her the courage to go after her tennis dreams and, even more dramatically, the confidence to let go of tennis to pursue *other* dreams. She is a tremendous advertisement for the power of Crowe's coaching skills and the Brené Brown mindset approach. Barty is that rare person capable of achieving enormous success without apparently being ensnared in its moral and philosophical traps. But here's a curious thing. It turns out that a proportion of Crowe's 'high performing individuals' are precisely those elite corporate leaders we have been talking about, including senior executives in Australian banks. They are not in the same league as the global tech overlords, but they significantly influence the shape of our lives through advertising, marketing, social media and strategic sponsorships.

In Fyfe's account, Crowe himself made the point that we each need to control our own story, 'because otherwise "the three biggest storytellers on the planet"—the news media ("predicated on negativity"), the advertising industry ("predicated on shame"), and social media ("predicated on social comparison and perfectionism")—will do it for you'.[21] Which must make for an interesting discussion between him and his corporate clients who are, after all, highly paid to flog just those products and services that capitalise on our pain, shame and responsiveness to social comparison. It seems ironic that Ben Crowe is helping corporate leaders become more authentic, vulnerable and connected while the rest of us remain at the mercy of the insecure, grasping, shallow society they lead and sustain.

But perhaps there isn't anything odd about this at all. If they are to retain good staff and keep their customers, our corporations know they need to look like they care about being authentic and empathetic and humble, and be seen to be trying to create safe, inclusive and diverse workplaces. Even if it is mainly for show, and even if their senior executive cohort is still mostly straight white men and some white women, many of whom went to leading private schools. CEOs and executives are being taught how to use the language of Brené Brown, and perhaps it doesn't matter to them whether they believe it or not.

In such a topsy-turvy world, we should not be surprised that Ash Barty's first big move after her retirement from tennis to 'follow her dreams' was to take up a new role at telecommunications giant Optus, with the improbable title of 'chief inspiration officer'. Look out for Barty inspiring you to be more connected and true to yourself and follow all your dreams, oh, and to buy your communications products and services from Optus. Because neoliberalism sees your earnest desire to live by 21st-century virtues, and promptly, efficiently and shamelessly monetises it.

MY TRUTH OR YOURS?

It used to be well understood that in democracies we were all entitled to our own opinions but not to our own facts. Now it appears we are all entitled to our own truth, to My Truth, which may or may not be based on fact but is wholly freighted with feelings. What a disastrous idea.

It was Stephen Colbert who in 2005 coined the term 'truthiness' in his Comedy Central satire *The Colbert Report*, in which he cast himself as a stupid but enthusiastic right-wing talk-show host and champion of Republican causes. George W Bush was US president at that time, and truthiness meant, according to Colbert, 'Believing something that feels true, even if it isn't supported by fact.' Articulating this trend through comedy provided a useful insight into a frightening development in US political life. It attested to the dumbness of the then president and the increasing ignorance and credulousness of the American people.

By 2016, Stephen Colbert was host of *The Late Show* in his own right on CBS. With the rise of Donald Trump as the Republican candidate for the presidency, Colbert brought back his old satirical right-wing persona to deliver a new monologue, updating his thoughts on the collapse of truth in American politics. 'Just to remind you,' he said, 'eleven years ago, I invented a word: truthiness … Truthiness comes from the gut because brains are over-rated.' On-screen came an image of a ranting Donald Trump. Colbert nodded approvingly towards the image. 'Naturally I admire this man. In fact, I see myself in him!' He continued: 'Truthiness has to feel true but Trumpiness doesn't even have to do that! In fact, many Trump supporters don't believe his wildest promises, and they don't care … And if he doesn't have to keep his wildest promises that means he can say anything.'[22]

On the *Salon* website last year, looking back at Colbert's speech, Sophia McClennen noted that the difference between 2005 and 2016 was that, in the Bush era, there was still a chance that the public cared about the actual facts, whereas now, 'in the Trump era, his fans have no interest whatsoever in the truth. They can learn that their candidate's statements are only true or mostly true twelve percent of the time and simply not care.'[23]

Colbert's underlying analysis of both truthiness and Trumpiness was that there was a rising resistance to science and reason, and a growing societal reliance upon feelings as a sufficient guide to belief and behaviour. In 2006, in an interview with Nathan Rabin, Colbert explained the powerfully circular and self-referential qualities particular to truthiness: 'It's not only that I *feel* it to be true, but that *I* feel it to be true. There's not only an emotional quality, but there's a selfish quality.'[24] And by 2010, he saw no end to the truthiness trend, telling *The New York Times*: 'I doubt that many people in American politics are acting on the facts. Everybody on both sides is acting on the things that move them emotionally the most.'[25]

Which brings us to the 'progressive' version of truthiness: My Truth. But first, it is useful to distinguish between this negative trend and a related positive one. Colonial history has until very recently been told by the victors, who inevitably made themselves the heroes of their own tales. Today, historians in Australia and elsewhere are correcting the old records by uncovering more facts, weighing the facts differently and incorporating the experiences of the losers of history: the colonised, the excluded, the enslaved and the marginalised. By telling the old stories afresh, with more and better information, they are working towards new understandings of historical truth.

One fine example is *The Anarchy: The East India Company, Corporate Violence and the Pillage of an Empire* (2019). William Dalrymple draws upon the East India Company's records and Persian-language sources, eyewitness accounts in private letters, and diaries for his fresh history of the firm. In his rounded retelling, the tale of benign British enterprise and colonisation in India becomes a tragedy for millions due to unbridled greed.

In *Making Australian History* (2022), Anna Clark charts the changing course of Australian history-telling. Historians still consult the 'official' histories, but also Indigenous histories, oral histories, poetry and fiction, family histories and more. As Clark says, 'Contact art on the rock face can be as historical as the writings of the colonists.'[26] By this, she means history is still told through close attention to evidence and reason while untainted by the colonial mindset of the past.

The My Truth syndrome, by contrast, arises from feelings. In early 2023, Britain's Prince Harry gave numerous interviews to promote his autobiography *Spare*. He freely betrayed the privacy of his family, attributed malign motives to other people's actions, and portrayed himself as a victim of his own dreadful life. This was a classic My Truth moment, worthy of the satire that followed. But the rise of My Truth matters, not because of a few high-profile individuals with an overattachment to their own feelings, but because an emphasis on feelings over facts poses dangers for democracy.

In 1985, Milan Kundera, recalling the 1968 Soviet invasion, related the weirdly 'sentimental' nature of the conquest. On one occasion, Russian infantrymen assured him, as they stopped and searched his car, 'You must realize we love the Czechs. We love you!' Kundera was not warmed by these sentiments. On the contrary. As Kundera puts it:

> When feelings supplant rational thought, they become the basis for an absence of understanding, for intolerance; they become, as Carl Jung has put it, 'the superstructure of brutality'. Man cannot do without feelings, but the moment they are considered values in themselves, criteria of truth, justifications for kinds of behaviour, they become frightening.[27]

On the broader effect on his life under Soviet occupation, Kundera said, 'When this weight of rational irrationality fell on my country, I felt an instinctive need to breathe deeply of the spirit of the post-Renaissance West.' That's why, when someone offered him the chance to write a stage play based on a novel by Fyodor Dostoevsky, Kundera declined. What irritated him about the venerated Russian writer was what Kundera called the *climate* of Dostoevsky's novels, 'a universe where everything turns into feeling; in other words, where feelings are promoted to the rank of value and truth'. Instead, Kundera decided to write a stage adaptation of a novel by the French Enlightenment champion Denis Diderot, the entrepreneur behind that great pro-science, pro-democratic project, the *Encyclopédie*—a document founded on a commitment to verifiable facts.[28]

In our modern world of vaccine deniers, conspiracy theorists and excitable coup participants, I find myself deeply uneasy. Good-hearted people want to respectfully include everyone in the conversation and give each of us a chance to have our say. There's a great welcoming of voices from all quarters, and a willingness to honour each individual's 'lived experience'. But this can only work if we cleave to some fundamental principles.

Once upon a time, Truthfulness was a virtue on the snakes and ladders board. It wasn't particularly complex. Indeed, it was crudely simple. This virtue didn't require any special nuance, or explication, or moral expertise. You either told a lie or you told the truth. Every sane person knew the difference. The present-day elevation of feelings over facts, the privileging of My Truth over the unvarnished truth, on the other hand, is a clear danger to democracy, whether it comes from the left or the right. We must resist it—yes, even if it hurts people's feelings. Because there are more than feelings at stake.

In 2020, historian Timothy Snyder produced a powerful little book called *On Tyranny: Twenty Lessons from the Twentieth Century*. Lesson number ten is 'Believe in Truth'. Snyder says plainly: 'To abandon facts is to abandon freedom. If nothing is true then no one can criticise power because there is no basis on which to do so … Post-truth is pre-fascism.'[29]

And we would do well to memorise this refrain from Nobel Peace Prize–winning journalist Maria Ressa: 'Without facts you can't have truth. Without truth you can't have trust. Without these three things, we have no shared reality, cannot solve problems, and have no democracy.'[30]

SELF-CARE: DON'T CARE

A new creature has arisen in our democracies: the self-described sovereign citizen. These individuals are not thankful for the benefits they derive from life in an organised community. They despise the security, prosperity and justice that permits them to flourish and realise their potential. Instead, they focus on the deprivations imposed upon them by the coercive mechanics of government. They renounce citizenship of their political community and declare themselves immune to its laws, while enjoying all their protections.

Once thought confined to the crazy backblocks of America, sovereign citizens have emerged on the highways of Australia where the great evil imposed upon them, apparently, is road rules. It seems they also dislike vaccinations, climate change (which they deny), gun laws and paying their taxes. They call it liberty, but of course it's an elevation of selfishness. It is a stand against the communalism that sustains us all, and in particular a stand against the concessions and contributions we make to live in our democracy. Self-denial on the snakes and ladders board may no longer be regarded as a virtue, but the truth is that most citizens still practise self-denial enthusiastically.

Parents give up their Saturdays to organise team sports for the kids. Retirees work with Vinnies or the Salvos. Working people donate to charities and worthwhile causes. Church groups coordinate fundraising and charity drives. Women still carry the weight of caring across society: caring for their parents, their children, their grandchildren, besides working in the underpaid 'caring' professions of teaching, nursing and aged care. The trade union movement coordinates collective action, and individuals join in and forgo the chance to make beneficial private trade-offs with their employers to protect the interests of the group. More people are choosing a sustainable pattern of living that repudiates consumerism and is better for the planet: they buy less, fly less, change their energy use, give up their cars. There are riches to be found in resiling from consumption, in the return to things handmade, recycled and homemade, knitting and sewing, work in community gardens. It reminds me of Orwell's version of the English private life.

The direct motivations may vary, and people may consciously be driven by love of family or community or hope for future generations as much as the abstract idea of democracy. But these are all ways in which people enact positive citizenship. They do so in the optimistic belief that with a little effort and self-sacrifice, we can all make things better.

Yet there's a strong counterforce at work in our society. If, nearly a hundred years ago, as the snakes and ladders board tells us, Self-Denial was a virtue and Vanity a vice, then today, Self-Denial is not only *not* a virtue, it is regarded as a somewhat embarrassing affectation. A tasteless gesture of moral excess. At the very least, a social solecism in an era dominated by the emollients of self-love, self-esteem and, most of all, Self-Care.

Of course, what is called Self Care in the modern sense is not just about lifestyle moderation and following the latest health and medical advice, all of which require some self-discipline and self-denial. Self-Care is instead a declaration of self-centredness as a virtue. It's certainly good for business: too much self-denial would dangerously undermine the entire neoliberal premise that insists upon consumption and self-gratification.

That's why we all need our Me-Time. It's nothing to be ashamed of. On the contrary. A New Year's email arrived in my inbox from an upmarket health resort: 'This is your sign that it's time to be selfish!' Recently, my local discount pharmacy chain, Priceline, ran 'A Festival of YOU!' with its latest make-up offers. 'You deserve to be CELEBRATED!' the advertise-ments said. They wanted to give me some 'well deserved bliss'. How did they know I deserved such bliss? Because we are *all* so very deserving.

Women friends of mine have told me that this self-care message is helpful to them. It makes them feel they have permission to do a little more for themselves in a world in which they are expected, as a matter of course, to do the emotional and often literal heavy lifting for family and friends. Under the banner of self-care, they can avoid feeling guilty when they take time out to book a massage or join a yoga class. But here's my question: why should they feel guilty at all? Why should they carry the burden unaided? Wouldn't it make sense for our society to better care for them in the form of higher wages and improved social support?

There's another reason why self-care is a regrettable must. It's a practical need in a world in which it is a crime to get old, by which I mean to look old. Even death is less embarrassing than being wrinkled. So your pocket is drained in the effort to hold back the tidal wave of your own decay, and to hang on to your fast-fading economic relevance in the neoliberal world. Sometimes, self-care feels more like self-loathing.

In corporate circles—certainly on LinkedIn— standards are even higher. It's not enough today to be clean and neat and appear relatively sane. Self-Care requires that the elites are whippet-thin, tight-skinned and in supreme mental health. It becomes a demanding discipline involving trainers and exercise equipment and dentists and nutrition- ists and cosmeticians and surgeons, not to mention therapists and mindset coaches. This level of self-care is so costly it is a virtue accessible only to the well-off. While rich people will have the financial resources and time to preserve their youthful looks and wiry bodies, poor people are more likely to be fat and ill-nourished and to make poor health choices. That consigns them by default to the un-Virtue column.

I've spent a fair bit of time going back and forth to inner-city hospitals. There's always one old guy—or at least he looks old—sitting in a wheelchair outside the hospital's front entrance, warming himself in a patch of sunlight. Skinny-legged in his hospital gown, he has an intravenous drip-line stand by his side, an oxygen mask hanging off his face, and a rogue cigarette in his wavering hand. I don't know what this guy has been through. I don't know if cigarettes, compared to the alternatives he's tried, represent his last-ditch effort at emotional self-care. One thing I'm sure of is that his life has been a lot harder than mine. As he takes a drag on his fag and utters another deep and fathomless cough, he is in every conceivable way a disgrace to the self-care mantra. He's a waste of taxpayers' money, he is a drain on the healthcare system, he's wilfully self-destructive.

It would be interesting to consider what the sovereign citizen might make of this guy. Perhaps he or she would despise him, living off others, passively accepting the hospital regimen, no doubt agreeing to the injections of toxic substances manufactured by the deep state. Or perhaps this guy is himself a sovereign citizen, brought by circumstance to the final indignity of public health.

As for me, I want to live in a society where we care for each other as well as ourselves, including those who've never done a moment's self-care. Without that balancing commitment, Self-Care as a virtue is just another way to erode the communal spirit that sustains our democracy.

VIRTUES VERSUS DEMOCRACY

You may think I am devoting energy in these pages to critiquing benign virtues, generally espoused by progressive, rational and decent people, when I should, in fact, be lamenting the bigoted, racist obsessions of the far right. But it is precisely because of the right-wing resurgence that I write this. If we are to combat this growing anti-democratic blight, we need to acknowledge where and how our 21st-century virtues are increasingly, if unwittingly, aiding the extreme right-wing agenda. Without the framework of a widely shared civic concept of virtue, democracy is weakened by neglect and default. Here is where right-wing politicians flourish, harnessing alienated people in our mass society, preaching the simple, unifying ideas of nationalism, government conspiracies, violence and follower-culture, as they seek to convert these disaffected individuals into extremist mobs. Donald Trump is a symptom, not a cause.

Brené Brown and others like her, with their self-first messages, may well lend courage to those who are fighting to overcome historic shame, exclusion and fear. There is clearly some positive link between the elevation of Authenticity as a virtue and resurgent calls for tolerance and inclusion. But where there is progress on tolerance, I also see a frightening rise in intolerance. A great deal of it, worryingly, comes from the left. As a writer I notice it in the creeping curtailment of freedom in the arts, and especially in writing and literature. These days in the publishing industry, for example, we find a new category of expert: the sensitivity reader. What a deceptively benign job title. The sensitivity reader's job is to read the text of a book and spy out examples of 'insensitive' language that may offend someone.

Consider the case of English author Anthony Horowitz. Among his many artistic achievements, Horowitz is the creator of *Foyle's War*, the beloved TV series about a British police officer striving to enforce the rule of law, protect civil rights and preserve humanity during and after World War II. Some time ago, Horowitz completed a new novel. Given that he was a British author writing for an American audience, Horowitz's publisher raised the idea of a 'sensitivity reading'. Like most authors, Horowitz wanted to please his publisher, so he agreed. The manuscript was duly passed to the sensitivity reader, who picked up on a plot point involving a Native American character (acting as a doctor in a play) who murders someone with a scalpel. Horowitz was informed that the word 'scalpel' should be removed, because it sounded too much like 'scalping' and could cause offence. Horowitz pointed out that the word 'scalpel' 'comes from the Latin word *scalpellus* (from *scalpere*, to cut) and has nothing to do with scalping, which derives from the Middle English word *scalpe*, meaning the top of the head'. Never mind that. Horowitz was advised to replace the word 'scalpel' with 'surgical instrument'. Crime fiction fans will no doubt agree with me that this is a sadly inferior term for a murder weapon. Horowitz complied but felt bad enough about this experience to write a rueful article for *The Spectator*.[31]

Of course, it is not uncommon for writers to show their manuscripts to trusted readers who can advise on nuance and language. And in this age of vulnerability and offence, a sensitivity reading may well be a sensible option to have on standby if an author requests it. But if even Horowitz feels obliged to comply with top-down pressure on his words, imagine what is happening to writers further down the literary ladder.

We are all rightly horrified by recent developments in America, particularly in Governor Ron DeSantis's Florida, where the wholesale censorship of books and art is underway. DeSantis is also attempting to wipe out the teaching of the African American experience and ban classroom discussions on health and sexuality. These horrors in the

United States, perpetrated by the right, should not blind us to emerging anti-democratic risks from the left. On the contrary. With the noble rationale of protecting the vulnerable and fostering inclusion, global publishers have decided it is acceptable to rewrite works by dead writers like Enid Blyton and Roald Dahl, eliminating egregious terms and phrasing that 'might' offend. I don't imagine for a moment that these publishers are motivated by anything more than profit, by the way, but that is no excuse. It is a wholesale trashing of artistic integrity.

More than this, as Anna Clark has reminded us, novels and stories are historical artefacts. They teach us that the past was a different country, that writers and artists we admire can also hold horrible views, that we are all products of our time and place. They invite us to contemplate that progress is possible and so is decline. The point of educating children, exposing them to literature and attitudes of different kinds, is to help them grow up, not to hold them suspended, in the name of their innocence, like flies in the aspic of historical lies.

A friend of mine recently remarked that, thankfully, these days there seem to be fewer reports of controversial speakers being 'cancelled' or 'uninvited' from university podiums and literary festivals. I suspect universities and festival organisers are quietly conducting their own sensitivity readings prior to sending out invitations. Easier to perform censorship in advance and avoid all the trouble. But censorship conducted discreetly behind the scenes should alarm and frighten us at least as much as government-mandated censorship. With these anonymous, unaccountable censors, we aren't even offered the democratic option of challenging their decisions or voting them out.

The broader risk is an undermining of the Enlightenment. I don't think it is unreasonable to remind ourselves of the worst that has happened and could happen. Such as the excesses of the Cultural Revolution in China from 1966 to 1976, when teenagers informed on their own parents who were guilty of nothing more than the crime of scholarly interests. Or the most radical period of the French Revolution, from 1792 to 1794, when revolutionaries killed thousands, rewrote the calendar and closed down the churches. The French revolutionary leader Maximilian Robespierre openly declared that terror and virtue were bound together.

As 2022 drew to a close, the poet, writer and biographer Mark Mordue offered this poignant assessment of the current state of affairs:

Art as something free-roaming and restorative, challenging and provocative as much as loving or pleasing … felt endangered. A bizarre counter-force, masked as 'goodness', threatened to moralise creative work out of any shadow or complexity, attempting to tame artists inside the safe houses of affirmation and acceptability … I don't think any artist worth their weight can accept this limit or service such approvals. Give me the best of heaven and hell in your work. And I will make my own way between them, inspired by your aim towards the truth.[32]

When writers, thinkers and artists are confined to their 'lived experience' lanes or limited by artificial moral delicacy in the scope and content of their work, we will all be morally, culturally and intellectually poorer. We won't get Heaven or Hell, just a sad Purgatory of cultural blandness. And worse. Once a society gets into the habit of controlling its writers and artists, we enter a realm that totalitarians of all stripes would find very comfortable indeed. It was when his books were banned in Czechoslovakia in 1975 that Kundera knew the worst had happened and left for exile in France.

Still, the excesses of modern inclusion do sometimes jolt people into laughter and a burst of common sense. An update to the famous *The Associated Press Stylebook* made the world chuckle in late January 2023. In the modern spirit of sensitivity, the *Stylebook* publicly recommended against 'general and often dehumanising "the" labels such as the poor, the mentally ill, the French, the disabled, the college educated'. Hang on, the *college educated*? And what, the *French*? *New York Times* columnist Nicholas Kristof wrote a short article about it, concluding with this point: 'I fear that our linguistic contortions, however well meant, aren't actually addressing our country's desperate inequities or achieving progressive dreams but rather are creating fuel for right-wing leaders aiming to take the country in the opposite direction.'[33]

The larger point is this: liberal democracies are not majoritarian. They provide space for individual freedoms of speech, mind and heart. Even for deeply tasteless and unlikeable expressions of those freedoms, whether from the right or the left. I'm not saying it's easy to strike the right balance. But if we accept, say, the right of religious institutions like the Christian and Islamic churches to exist, with their mysticism and sexism and homophobia and conservativism, then there is no point in punishing those churches or their adherents for the very discriminations that define their faith.

It's equally difficult when we are talking about the rights of parents over their children. But if you accept the right of these intolerant institutions and individuals to exist—and in a liberal democracy, that is exactly what we must do—there is little point in demanding wholesale that they publicly undermine their own values to prove a point. At the very least, we should accept that these are not simple questions with easy answers.

Does that mean that we who are liberal progressives accept that tolerance is merely widespread but not, alas, universal? Yes, because that's how liberal democracies work. We can and should debate where we draw the lines, and we should be open to persuasion on where those lines are drawn. And yes, progress sometimes requires a brave political push instead of waiting around for majority support. But I maintain this: we have to tolerate a certain amount of intolerance within any true democracy. We have to accept that the benefits of a stable, well-functioning, ordered community will both override and underwrite the individual freedoms we enjoy. We do this to protect democracy itself. Which is why we must forestall or reverse any well-meaning 'progressive' creep of ideological oppression. Because we may inadvertently be paving the way for more oppression, of an even worse kind.

LINKEDIN: NEOLIBERALISM'S PORTAL

It's time to talk about LinkedIn. You may wonder why I'm writing about it at all. Who cares about some boring corporate networking site?

LinkedIn certainly started out, in 2003, as a professional networking site. It was a place where big corporations and their recruitment firms could advertise jobs; where marketing managers and HR professionals promoted themselves for their next role; where graphic designers, advertisers, copywriters, and speechwriters like me, could promote their wares. LinkedIn was a place where people put themselves forward as competent, sane and employable. Over time, however, LinkedIn has turned into a Brené Brownian/ neoliberal wonderland. It is the place you go to for the best of all possible worlds, where corporate vision, whole hearts, great work and a fulfilled life coexist in perfect equipoise, with good times and teamwork leading to virtuous riches and success for all. On LinkedIn, it's all about being authentic, honest and transparent; promoting diverse, inclusive and caring workplaces; and respecting work–life balance— while at the same time bringing our whole selves to work. As long as you know these secrets to success, life is a generous feast of mutual backscratching, humblebragging and virtue signalling.

And a lot of nonsense. I saw one profile on LinkedIn the other day where the bloke described his professional skill set as 'Delivering change through experience and knowledge'. A toddler's babble would be more meaningful. When people on LinkedIn say coyly that they are struggling to overcome the curse of 'imposter syndrome', I often suspect the reason they feel like imposters is because, in fact, they are.

In this self-congratulatory world, LinkedIn specialises in awards nights. Awards for everyone and everything: marketing prowess, digital excellence, online security, diversity and inclusion, regional innovation. Photos of middle managers in evening wear, smiling broadly and holding a plaque in a hotel ballroom. There's usually a group photo because, really, it's all about the team. Everyone is so humbled by the recognition but also so proud and grateful, and let's download our selfies and videos for the office website so everyone in the office can see how well we are all doing, oh, and our clients can too. Because good people will want to work with other good people.

Philanthropy on LinkedIn is an even better opportunity to show virtue. People are always running, swimming, cycling or trekking somewhere photogenic for a cause. This is fantastic because it combines philanthropy with self-care. The HR guy crosses the finish line, exhausted and elated by his fundraising efforts, and everyone is on standby to take videos and photos and tell his followers that the $10 000 he raised by keeping himself exceptionally fit is now going to some children's hospital ward near you. And guess what? His fantastically supportive company will now DOUBLE the charitable contribution. Win-win! The idea of quietly transferring funds to a worthy cause doesn't seem to occur to anyone.

The current owner of LinkedIn is Microsoft. The foot soldiers promoting the LinkedIn ideology are HR professionals in big corporates armed with psychology degrees. These are the true carriers of Brené Brownism—the language of modern HR is 100 per cent Brownian. Your demonstrations of authenticity, vulnerability and, most of all, humility are all highly prized. Until they make you redundant, when you will be reminded by your HR person of your obligations under your company's draconian confidentiality and non-disclosure agreements as they push you out the door.

In this Panglossian world, small Chekhovian tragedies unfold. Amanda, for example, posts one evening that she is so grateful for the wonderful journey she has had with company X. She's a little nervous about what lies ahead but really excited for it. She doesn't say she has been made redundant, but she doesn't need to because everyone knows company X has just sacked 10 000 people after its poor results. 'Excited about the journey,' she says, which really means, 'Rather nervous about what may happen next.' Amanda then gets fifteen likes, plus three comments wishing her 'Good luck' and 'All the best' and 'Exciting times!' She replies that she is really humbled by all the support she is getting and is looking forward to the next stage in her journey.

A few weeks later we again hear from Amanda, who has changed her descriptor on LinkedIn to 'Content Creator'. She tells everyone she is excited to announce she is achieving her lifelong dream of creating her own podcast, which is all about how people can overcome adversity to find career success and personal fulfilment. After she has released two episodes, Amanda upgrades her work title to 'Founder/Content Creator'.

Not long after this, Amanda's tone changes: 'I don't normally like to post anything personal on this site, but I'm not going to lie, it's been a tough time. I've been shortlisted for a few roles but haven't got them. I've been struggling, but I know if I stay positive things will work out. Everything happens for a reason.' Amanda gets ten likes and another trio of comments: 'Stay Strong' and 'Love your honesty' and 'You got this!'

Soon after, Amanda is both proud and humbled to announce she has found her dream job with a mid-tier financial services firm as a transformation and change specialist. She is excited because she really admires this firm's passion for inclusivity and diversity and celebrating everyone's unique talents. She already knows it's a place where she can bring her whole authentic self to work. She thanks everyone who has helped her along the way and can't wait to see where this next adventure leads her.

There are many Amandas on LinkedIn, and while they may or may not be very literate, or good at their jobs, they have undoubtedly mastered the language of modern neoliberal virtue, as they faithfully serve the propaganda needs of the virtuous corporation.

It was not always like this. Back in 1963, Saul Bellow was reflecting ruefully on the high moral standards expected of writers like himself, and he contrasted this with the free pass given to the big capitalist American corporations. No-one, he said, asked a big corporation to demonstrate virtue. He added: 'It may, if it is public spirited, hire an advertising firm to explain how much good it is doing' but it 'doesn't make sweeping moral claims. It simply says: capitalism is good for you. We are tough energetic realists and that is as God and the founding fathers meant it to be.'[34]

Today's public corporation does make sweeping moral claims, with mission statements of breathtaking overreach. LinkedIn is where capitalism masquerades as a series of noble causes, where the modern virtues can be and are being coopted to advance the neoliberal agenda. And with the corporatisation of so many formerly public or community organisations, including sporting codes, things are only getting worse.

LinkedIn's disguising of the corporate world's lack of virtue is helped by a convenient matter of etiquette:

it is considered poor form to include 'political' discourse on the platform. This rule is taken so seriously that it is regarded as a faux pas to have any form of morality at all. One individual with a background in corporate relations posted with pride on LinkedIn that they were heading overseas to a senior role in the national tourism promotion body of a nation with one of the world's worst recent human rights records. No matter. Hundreds of former colleagues and contacts rushed to praise this move. It was all 'Congratulations' and 'A new adventure!' and 'They are lucky to have you!' One commentator gently hinted at an uncomfortable truth: would not this role inevitably involve glossing up the image of a nation with a terrible human rights record? Undeterred, the person sent a cheery reply: 'But things are changing and the place is opening up!' Right then.

Which reminds me. In her profile on Ben Crowe, Melissa Fyfe noted that her conversation with the mindset coach was taking place as Crowe prepared to deliver a keynote speech to the leaders of health insurer Bupa at a Novotel in Melbourne's CBD. As Crowe calmed his nerves before going on stage to speak, he shared with Fyfe—and us—his own vulnerability and relatability: 'I'm imperfect but I'm worthy and I've got something to say.'[35] Crowe may be imperfect, but Bupa has not always been worthy.

Yes, the company talks a good game. In a perfect parade of corporate neoliberal/Brené Brownian virtues, Bupa says on its website:

> Our purpose, helping people live longer, healthier, happier lives and making a better world, is more than just words on a page. It's a promise to our customers to change lives for the better. It inspires our culture and is brought to life every day by our people.[36]

Let's see. In 2016, Bupa admitted it had spent five years lying to its customers, telling them that rejections of their insurance claims had been 'determined by a medical practitioner', when in fact Bupa had disallowed 7740 insurance claims without a doctor's review at all.[37] In 2020, the Federal Court ordered that Bupa pay $6 million in penalties for making misleading representations and wrongly accepting payments for 'extra services'—that is, services not provided at all, or only partly delivered—to the residents of twenty of its aged-care homes.[38] And then there was the revelation of 2021, when Bupa admitted underpaying 18 000 former and current employees by up to $75 million.[39]

So much for happier customers, building a better society and caring for their people. But on LinkedIn, you will rarely find a word about that kind of thing, because to call out hypocrisy or exploitation would be to bring 'politics' to the platform. Simply Not Done.

FROM CLASS VIRTUES TO
PERSONAL LABELS

When I was growing up, like many other children, I was instinctively on the side of the heroic virtues, especially when I read my dad's old Scarlet Pimpernel books. The eponymous hero was Sir Percy Blakeney, an eighteenth-century English baronet who risked his life, time and again, to rescue French nobility from the guillotine during the French Revolution. He represented the epitome of the aristocratic warrior class, with his wit, joie de vivre and gallantry, combined with a fervent attachment to personal honour, even if it might cost his life.

The Scarlet Pimpernel was created in the nineteenth century by a nostalgic Hungarian aristocrat, Baroness Orczy, whose family had fallen on hard times. In her Pimpernel books, she was writing into a long tradition whereby aristocrats idealised themselves and their class, commissioning art, architecture and magnificent public events to weave a captivating romance around their virtues. As a child, it never occurred to me that these aristocratic virtues were unavailable to the lower classes, or that aristocrats saw themselves as the sole carriers of any virtues that really mattered.

With modern industrialisation, the rural peasants became the urban working class. They were and are characterised by virtues like Loyalty, Solidarity, Community and Humour. Of necessity, there is a focus on present needs rather than future prospects, plus suspicion of governments and institutions. This, combined with poverty and exclusion from civic power, has also meant a certain historical tolerance for lawlessness.

The bourgeois virtues were traditionally ones of Thrift, Work, Sobriety and a capacity for Delayed Gratification. Democracy was embraced because the bourgeoisie valued individual freedoms assured by a stable political system and guaranteed by rule of law. The rise in the novel as an art form in the nineteenth century was almost entirely coincidental with the growth of this new class, preoccupied as it was by money, respectability and status, and inevitably undercut by secrecy and hypocrisy.

The late eighteenth- and nineteenth-century Romantic movement saw a powerful reaction against these materialist bourgeois values. The Romantic poets and artists, musicians and philosophers—including the rather eccentric Nietzsche—generally cultivated their individualism, and subscribed to idealist social visions, love of nature and big heroic ideas. They eschewed the social self to concentrate on the mysteries and inner workings of the heart. They were so successful at attacking the middle class that, until very recently, to call someone or something 'bourgeois' was a term of abuse meaning small-minded and conservative. But the term appears to have been repurposed, at least in some circles. A friend of mine who casts for reality TV shows tells me it's common for young wannabe celebrities, when asked about their hopes and dreams, to say they really want to 'live bougie'. What they mean by 'bougie', it seems, has nothing to do with work, propriety and stability, but comforts and luxuries, photogenic spaces, and the latest technology and entertainment.

What it means to be an individual is changing too. Today, it is possible to *claim* an authentic identity as an act of self-affirmation. I have heard of more than a few calls to mothers from teenage and young adult children announcing, 'Mum, I'm queer, I hope you are not upset.' Or 'I've realised I'm non-binary and you can call me Charlie.' Or 'You should know that I now call myself a person of colour.' The parental response, combining placation with resignation, is usually along the lines of, 'That's nice darling, see you at dinner.'

But I wonder what it means that young people feel such a strong need to label themselves like this at all, especially at their time of maximum unmet potentiality. It suggests a misguided faith that a label will magically solve the fundamental uncertainty that goes with being human. Here I also see the quest for Brené Brownian authenticity at work once again: a craving for it, even if it has to be defined or imposed from without rather than generated from within. Yet labels can be misleading or disingenuous as much as illuminating. Say I tell you that I am a 'cishet (cisgender heterosexual) white woman of privilege'. I thereby acknowledge the advantages I have in life while signalling my solidarity with others who are presently under-represented or disadvantaged. If I define myself as an 'ageing white woman', I am still acknowledging my privilege as a white woman but subtly highlighting my disadvantage as an ageing one.

I confess I have in the past allowed people who might have taken me for just another privileged white woman to know that my father was a butcher and my mother a typist. Yes, Dear Reader, I have played the class card. And done my complicated parents, and indeed myself, an injustice. I note here sadly that class has been demoted in public discourse, despite the fact that economic and social inequality remains the biggest source of disadvantage and the biggest opportunity for national democratic progress.

A label may be a form of public communication, but humans are not cans of tomatoes. The Australian Bureau of Statistics, in the 2021 Census, asked Australians to tick a box indicating either male, female or non-binary sex. This seemingly innocent item provoked so much confusion and dissent that the ABS had to admit the question did not yield sufficiently meaningful data to be useful. It did, however, yield numerous vivid alternative labels in the comments box, from agender, demiboy, gender fluid and non-binary gender, to transwoman, bisexual, gay, lesbian and pansexual, and some science-based labels such as intersex or 47XXY/Klinefelter syndrome.[40]

Yet even witty, novel or striking new definitions of the self can be reductive and diminishing as much as liberating. The more we are defined by category, the less we may be perceived, or even see ourselves, as whole, complex individuals. Philosopher Søren Kierkegaard put it this way: 'Once you label me, you negate me.'

We are now moving through an era of teeming and vivid diversity, with great possibilities for individual emancipation and civic participation. Younger Australians, globalised and multicultural, are ready to celebrate human difference in all its forms. They demand equal opportunity for people of all creeds and colours, inclusion in all aspects of life for people with disabilities, and acceptance of all the varieties of human sexuality. The risk is not that Australian society won't accept or embrace this diversity. All the evidence of recent years, including the success of the marriage equality vote and the joy of WorldPride, suggests we will. But this future can only be assured if we agree that the wellbeing of the community comes prior to the self-absorbed individual; that we move forward as responsible citizens within a shared reality, with an eye to the democratic whole as much as its diverse parts.

INFLATABLE VIRTUES: EMPATHY AND HUMILITY

'Empathy' is a relatively new word in the virtue lexicon. Coined in about 1895, its use took off dramatically in the twentieth century. 'Pity' was the commonly used term for many centuries, with its original meaning linked to the Latin word 'pious', meaning 'duty'. Nietzsche thought pity was an appallingly patronising sentiment and damned it for all time. The more acceptable Latinate word 'compassion' and its Greek sibling 'sympathy' share with 'empathy' the Greek root 'pathos', meaning simply 'with feeling'.

The word 'empathy' is for some reason now deemed superior in virtue content to any of the older ways of expressing much the same idea; that is, the idea of kindness towards another human being who is suffering. I assume it is considered superior because it implies something more than just being kind, more than being by someone's side when they are in trouble. Rather than looking at another human being's suffering from the outside and doing what you can for them, empathy means imagining yourself in their place, feeling what they feel, sharing their grief. But if pity is patronising, empathy is presumptuous. In this self-centred age, empathy has the clear benefit of enabling the individual to put themselves centrestage in the drama of another's pain: I have an image of someone forcibly climbing into another person's shoes.

It seems ironic to me that we should insist upon this idea of empathy at a time when we are also invited, more than ever before, to recognise each person's unique individuality and the very real differences between us. If we each feel our own joys and experience our sorrows in our own unique ways, how can we pretend to know what others feel?

In *Dare to Lead*, Brené Brown comes down strongly on the side of empathy. Sympathy is inadequate, she says, because it is feeling *for* other people, while empathy is feeling *with* them. Empathy means recognising that 'someone's in a deep well' and they are shouting out from the bottom, 'It's dark and scary down here.' Empathy, she says, means peering over the edge and saying, 'I see you,' then climbing down into the well with the suffering person. We are reminded of Nietzsche, the mountain climber, who warned that if you looked too long into the abyss, the abyss would surely look back into you. Brown qualifies her injunction differently: you shouldn't descend into the well if you don't have your own way out. No, no, that would be *enmeshment*. She doesn't need to remind us that self-care comes first.[41]

To explain the virtue of Empathy, Brown uses the example of the Me Too movement, saying that 'me too' are 'the two most powerful words when someone's in struggle'. But the Me Too movement is not about a vague fellow-feeling. It is about thousands, millions of women quite plainly declaring that, as a matter of fact, sexual harassment, assault and discrimination has happened to them, or to someone they know. In real life, not just in their warm-hearted imaginations.[42]

I pause here for the personal anecdote, which you may of course ignore as insufficiently evidential. For what it's worth, when I had eight months of gruelling breast cancer treatment, what I found so moving and delightful was that different friends and family members comforted me ('com' plus 'fort' literally meaning 'adding strength' to me) in very different ways. Far from putting themselves in my shoes, they looked to their own strengths and indeed their own pleasures as guides. Cooking friends made their favourite dishes and brought them around. My brother couldn't cook, but after work he'd go to his local delicatessen and buy delicious ready-made meals and deliver them to my front door. Another friend sent me a couple of books each month—she would scour second-hand bookshops and send me her beautifully curated choices. On the days I went into the office, a colleague made me laugh and bought me extravagant presents.

Empathy may be a nice feeling, but kindness demands and generates action.

The last thing I was hoping for was that other people would 'feel my feelings' with me: that would simply add to my own emotional burden. I would have felt stifled if anyone had wanted to cower with me in the bottom of my personal well of suffering. I am not other people, and they are not me. They don't feel my pain, and I cannot feel theirs. That's the beauty and mystery and sometimes the tragedy of the human condition: we share so much and yet we remain separate.

The idea of the empathetic leader is, of course, laughable. Naturally it is wildly popular on LinkedIn. Executive coaches solemnly extol this mode of leadership as (yet another) wave of the future. Brown's *Dare to Lead* is a management book for sale in the business section of my bookshop. But a leader really can't logically be hopping into the hearts and minds, not to mention the private wells, of each staff member and all of their customers and clients and stakeholders. Although I have come across CEOs who will try their best to imagine and anticipate every last feeling experienced by their company chair.

We don't need leaders who fixate on individual experiences and extrapolate policy from them. Nor do we need a philanthropic or charitable world where the focus is purely on responding to the most touching individual cases, those that evoke our 'empathetic' feelings. We need leaders who operate out of reason and who are, in the end, informed by boring old data and history and facts and statistics. A good heart matters, but a wise and well-informed head is essential. In the end, Empathy seems to me a vivid example of virtue inflation, where we hype up an ancient human concept with a fancier word that gives it more apparent gravitas, and that air of sympathetic alliance with the broken and vulnerable and well-dwelling, in the Brené Brownian mode.

A similar inflation issue pertains to Humility. To be 'humble' used to mean living as a low-status peasant, at the bottom of the social hierarchy, before the term morphed into its modern sense as a moral quality. The most interesting case study of this word in action was when Rupert Murdoch, owner of that egregious publication *News of the World*—the one that illegally trashed the privacy of numerous people—appeared before a British parliamentary committee in 2011 and said, 'This is the most humble day of my life.' I gnawed over that curious choice of the word 'humble' for some time. Murdoch is a literate man, and his prepared statement would have been carefully worked over by lawyers and advisers. I have no doubt it was his deliberate decision to use the slightly odd adjective 'humble' rather than 'humbling' or even 'humiliating'. I suspect Murdoch was in no way conceding that he humbly accepted the widespread censure of the actions of his business. I think he was saying quite honestly that he had been brought to the unexpected position of lowly penitent and it was a nasty shock.

Benjamin Franklin, one of the greatest of the American founding fathers, was also one of the first modern self-help gurus. In 1784, as part of an ongoing effort to improve his own character, he wrote down what he considered to be the key virtues: Temperance, Silence, Order, Resolution, Frugality, Industry, Sincerity, Justice, Moderation, Cleanliness, Tranquillity and Chastity. An alarmingly long list, with its intermingling of the Quaker and Puritan virtues he grew up with. Franklin then showed his work to a friend, who pointed out a glaring omission: perhaps the highly self-consequential writer might consider putting Humility on his list? Franklin added it but he had his doubts, stating 'even if I could conceive that I had completely overcome it, I should probably be proud of my humility'.[43]

People say they are humbled a lot these days, especially on LinkedIn, at one of those interminable awards nights. Nine times out of ten, this means that they consider themselves mighty successful but feel a need to perform modesty in order to be considered likeably relatable in modern life. A profession of humility should almost always be considered a humblebrag. La Rochefoucauld certainly thought so. He considered humility an elaborate trick, in which we feign submissiveness in order to feel even more superior to others.[44] My equation: modern humility equals pride plus an air of bashfulness.

The journalist Lynn Barber couldn't recall whether it was Gore Vidal or Christopher Hitchens who once said: 'I am a stranger to all forms of modesty, including the false.'[45] I'm not saying I automatically love a huge boaster, although I often do. It is a joy to be with people who are happy in themselves, delighted at what they have accomplished, who trust that your own ego is sufficiently well bolstered to cope if they share news of their successes with you. To me that feels like mutual respect, which is far better than either intrusive empathy or bogus humility. And isn't mutual respect a far better basis for friendship, solidarity and civic action in our democracy?

LOOKING BEYOND

I came across a modern snakes and ladders set the other day. At Officeworks, for less than $10, you'll find a brightly coloured version of the game. It has the same 100 squares, the same snakes and ladders motifs, the same possibility of a sudden rise or fall in competitive fortune as its forebears. But the updated game lacks the defining feature of the original: its morality lesson. There are no virtues and no sins. Perhaps it's all too hard. The makers seem to have decided it's less stressful to play life's game without any moral guidelines at all.

By now you may think I am entirely negative about Authenticity and the other modern virtues that are proselytised on LinkedIn. Not altogether. After all, God is dead and we are all trying to figure out what life is about, and how to find meaning, and how to feel that we are good people. As Saul Bellow said in his Nobel Prize Lecture in 1976, there is 'an immense, painful longing for a broader, more flexible, fuller, more coherent, more comprehensive account of what we human beings are, who we are, and what this life is for'.[46] But without the social and political context of democracy, the promoters and practitioners of the modern virtues I have described here will play into the hands of right-wingers and neoliberalism. Imagine if we just sleepwalked into Neo-Fascism. America still might. And we should not assume it could never happen in Australia.

After the Cold War ended in 1989, many rational people believed that totalitarianism as a viable project had been defeated; that the world, knowing what it did, could never again turn back. Political theorist Francis Fukuyama called this 'the end of history', with the universalisation of Western liberal democracy as the final form of human government.

But in 2016, Donald Trump became president of the United States. We saw him undertake a process of destroying American democracy by modern means, aided by the Russian Neo-Fascist kleptocracy. Instead of suppressing democratic debate by strict censorship, Trump, brilliantly understanding the power of social media, encouraged a tidal wave of competing voices to drown out the facts, to disable the truth, to confuse, misdirect, misinform and overwhelm American citizens. He actively fostered ignorance, incivility and cheating in American politics. He was cosy with tyrants around the world. He encouraged a violent uprising when he lost the 2020 election. He hasn't gone away, nor have his politics, nor has the risk to democracy in America and elsewhere. More of Authenticity or Humility or Vulnerability is not the answer. These are the inward-looking virtues that play right into the hands of both neoliberalism and Neo-Fascism.

In his *Crisis of Democratic Capitalism*, Martin Wolf calls for the return of some older virtues in the general population, and especially among elites, if democratic capitalism is to survive: 'Neither politics nor the economy will function without a substantial degree of honesty, trustworthiness, self-restraint, truthfulness and loyalty to shared political, legal and other institutions.'[47] Wolf's point is well made. But I can't help thinking that the future of democracy in Australia might be imagined in more optimistic terms. Why shouldn't we embrace the potential and contributions of all of our citizens, set the highest standards for facts and truth, demand the full accountability of leaders and the rule of law for all, and honour and fiercely protect freedom of thought and speech? We need settle for nothing less than a renewal of our national confidence, creativity and courage.

And if you still can't imagine what an heroically inspiring democratic future might look like, then look again.

Right now, the small, poor, Central European nation of Ukraine is fighting for its life against a monstrous invading Russia. Ukraine is an ancient culture but a young democracy, and its people want to live in peace and freedom and with a confident sense of long-term security. The Ukrainian president is a 45-year-old former comedian and actor who is inspiring the world with the best speeches since Winston Churchill in World War II. Most people assumed he would run away at the first sign of trouble. But in the early hours of Saturday, 26 February 2022, with the invasion just underway, President Volodymyr Zelensky filmed himself for his people and the world to see in front of the main church in Kyiv. 'I am here,' he said. 'We are not putting down arms. We will be defending our country, because our weapon is truth, and our truth is that this is our land, our country, our children, and we will defend all of this. That is it. That's all I wanted to tell you. Glory to Ukraine.'

The Ukrainian embassy in Britain later told CNN that President Zelensky had turned down an offer of evacuation from the United States. 'The fight is here; I need ammunition, not a ride,' Zelensky replied. Those words will go down in history.

I had finally signed up to Twitter, so I was in a position to follow developments in real time. I've since learnt of filmmakers, writers, poets, professors, surgeons, teachers, architects, men and women, fighting and dying for Ukraine's freedom and sovereignty. I've read of DJs swapping their green-sequinned jackets for army greens, ballet dancers losing their legs or their lives for their country. I've seen gatherings in villages where young people play music and dance as they work together to rebuild the shattered homes of individuals they have never met. I've read of old women in occupied villages bravely hiding ammunition under their beds so that, as they rush out to embrace liberating Ukrainian soldiers, they can hand over the precious bullets. I've seen images of young men dead, dying, legs blown off, eyes burnt out, being held tenderly by their comrades; they don't show us the bodies of the warrior women. I've learnt about the speed and ingenuity of Ukrainian fighters and civil society as they overcome each new obstacle, each new weapon, each new threat.

I was introduced via Twitter to young Dmytro, an engineer and amateur baker. When Russia invaded his land, he enlisted in the Ukrainian Army to defend it and simultaneously came out as a proud queer man, saying, 'I won't hide who I am anymore.' Why? 'Because all Ukrainians fight for our freedom of being unapologetically who we are.' He believes, it seems, that winning this fight for democracy against Vladimir Putin's dictatorship will provide the essential framework within which he truly can be himself.[48]

Some of the finest communications come from the Ukrainian Defence Force. Their messages are like nothing you've ever seen from any national defence operation. They are often hilariously rude to the Russians. Always inspiring. Sometimes visionary and poetic. Like this tribute to one handsome young soldier: 'Ihor Mitrov, Ukrainian poet and literary critic. Today he is a serviceman of the Ukrainian army. Ihor was born in Kerch, Crimea. Our poets are fighting against convicts and washing machine thieves. Our poets will win. Ukraine will win.'[49] In response, Mick Ryan, hardened Australian soldier and author of *War in the Future*, said: 'Easy to fall in love with a country, a democracy and a people that think—and fight—like this.'[50]

Timothy Snyder is a world expert on Ukraine. He is part of a passionate and tireless community of historians, foreign policy experts, soldiers and ordinary people from around the world who are backing Ukraine with all their hearts. Some of the Americans in this informal coalition see in the Ukrainian fight for democracy the high hopes, political savvy, fighting genius and advanced alliance-building skills that characterised the achievements of the American founding fathers in 1776, when they fought the British and created the American republic.

When we talk about the search for meaning, it is worth remembering that looking endlessly inwards is not the only or best way to find it. We can look out and beyond, to the something bigger than ourselves that is our democratic community.

This idea is expressed most powerfully in a poem by Walt Whitman, 'Song of Myself', that was first drafted in 1855 and revised in 1892. It begins with an outright expression of ego: 'I celebrate myself, and sing myself.' No humility here then. No vulnerability whatsoever. As the poem unfolds, we learn that this poet's self, so authentic, original and bright, is created not in isolation but through the overlapping, interweaving and embracing of all aspects of the democratic American way of life. With a cast of Americans of every hue, rank, status and religion, Whitman takes us in vivid images from east coast to west coast, from southerner to northerner, from agriculture to industry, through the cities and towns, the rural landscapes, the homes and shops; in fact, the whole of America is embraced, from the lights of the cosmos down to the delicate leaves of grass. The poem is filled with expressions of sexuality both heterosexual and homosexual. 'I contain multitudes,' Whitman cries out joyfully. And the paradox of this version of democracy is that only through this great human project can the promise of all its constituent individuals be achieved.

Every time an Australian government announces a new mental health scheme and fortunes to be spent on psychologists, I think to myself: that's all very well, but perhaps we would be better off focusing on the core things that will strengthen our democracy and the institutions that will allow our people to flourish—universal health care; universal high-quality education, public services and community goods; and genuine equality of opportunity. Then we might not need so many therapists.

Democracy can't survive on its own. It is under slow threat from the forces of neoliberalism and Neo-Fascism, and the terrible prospect of a nexus between the two. It can wither and die through disillusion and lack of care from a self-absorbed population. It can die of a thousand cuts, as Maria Ressa and others have warned us. Democracy needs infusions of energy and nourishment to thrive. As it fights back against a corrupt, totalitarian, invading Russia, Ukraine is fighting for us all.

Saul Bellow imagined there might be human qualities as yet undiscovered. I believe we will reveal those qualities—those virtues—not by looking inside ourselves but by looking out, not by encouraging our uniqueness or our weakness but by finding our shared strengths, and issuing a courageous, affirmative, collective *Yes*. When we do this, we might find that we can overcome all the challenges we face. And it may even be that the best is yet to come.

ACKNOWLEDGEMENTS

This book owes a great deal to conversations with my husband Syd Hickman. Thank you also to my first readers: my beloved late friend Gabrielle Carey, and Charlotte Wood, Vicki Hastrich and Tegan Bennett Daylight. A warm thank you to Jane Novak, my agent. Special thanks to Julia Carlomagno, Publisher at Monash University Publishing, and Paul Smitz, my generous and astute editor.

NOTES

1 François de la Rochefoucauld, *Maxims*, translated by Leonard Tancock, Penguin, Harmondsworth, 1959, p. 65.
2 William Dalrymple (@DalrympleWill), *Twitter*, 9 September 2022 (viewed May 2023).
3 Friedrich Nietzsche, *The Gay Science*, translated by Walter Kaufman, Vintage, New York, 1974, p. 223.
4 Brené Brown, 'The Power of Vulnerability', *TEDx*, Houston, 2010, https://www.ted.com/talks/brene_brown_the_power_of_vulnerability/comments/transcript (viewed May 2023).
5 Brené Brown, *Daring Greatly: How the Courage to Be Vulnerable Transforms the Way We Live, Love, Parent and Lead*, Penguin Random House, London, 2015.
6 Theodore Roosevelt, 'Citizenship in a Republic', speech at the Sorbonne, Paris, 23 April 1910.
7 Brené Brown, *Dare to Lead: Brave Work. Tough Conversations. Whole Hearts*, Vermilion, London, 2018.
8 Brené Brown, *The Gifts of Imperfection: Let Go of Who You Think You're Supposed to Be and Embrace Who You Are*, 10th anniversary edn, Random House, USA, 2020.
9 Harvard Business School, 'Authentic Leader Development', 2023, https://www.exed.hbs.edu/authentic-leader-development (viewed May 2023).
10 Lucinda Holdforth, *Why Manners Matter: The Case for Civilised Behaviour in a Barbarous World*, Random House, Sydney, 2007.

11 Anatole Broyard, 'Saul Bellow's World', *The New York Times*, 3 March 1984, https://archive.nytimes.com/www.nytimes.com/books/00/04/23/specials/bellow-fuchs.html?scp=3&sq=I%2520Will%2520Not%2520Let%2520You%2520Go&st=cse (viewed May 2023).

12 Nietzsche, *The Gay Science*, p. 303.

13 Hannah Arendt, *The Human Condition*, 2nd edn, University of Chicago Press, Chicago, 1988, p. 71.

14 George Orwell, 'England Your England', George Orwell's Library, 19 February 1941, https://orwell.ru/library/essays/lion/english/e_eye (viewed May 2023).

15 Philip Roth, 'In Defense of Intimacy: Milan Kundera's Private Lives', *The Village Voice*, 26 June 1984.

16 Philip Roth, 'Afterword: A Talk with the Author', in Milan Kundera, *The Book of Laughter and Forgetting*, Penguin, New York, 1983, p. 233.

17 George Monbiot, 'Neoliberalism: The Ideology at the Root of All Our Problems', *The Guardian*, 15 April 2016, https://www.theguardian.com/books/2016/apr/15/neoliberalism-ideology-problem-george-monbiot (viewed May 2023).

18 Martin Wolf, *The Crisis of Democratic Capitalism*, Penguin, London, 2023, pp. 218–19.

19 Amy Remeikis, 'Australia's Richest Captured 93% of Economic Growth between 2009 Financial Crisis and Covid, Paper Shows', *The Guardian*, 11 April 2023, https://www.theguardian.com/business/2023/apr/11/australias-richest-captured-93-of-economic-growth-between-2009-financial-crisis-and-covid-paper-shows (viewed May 2023).

20 Melissa Fyfe, 'Ash, Dylan, Dusty: Mindset Coach Ben Crowe Explains How He Makes Our Best Better', *The Sydney Morning Herald*, 25 June 2022, https://www.smh.com.au/national/ash-dylan-dusty-mindset-coach-ben-crowe-explains-how-he-makes-our-best-better-20220513-p5al8p.html (viewed May 2023).

21 Ibid.

22 Stephen Colbert, 'The Word: Trumpiness', *The Late Show with Stephen Colbert*, YouTube, 19 July 2016, https://www.youtube.com/watch?v=NqOTxl3Bsbw (viewed May 2023).

23 Sophia A McClennen, 'Colbert Goes after Trumpiness', *Salon*, 22 July 2016, https://www.salon.com/2016/07/22/colbert_goes_after_trumpiness_his_live_rnc_coverage_revives_the_comedy_of_the_colbert_report (viewed May 2023).

24 Nathan Rabin, 'Stephen Colbert', *AV Club*, 25 January 2006, https://www.avclub.com/stephen-colbert-1798208958 (viewed May 2023).

25 Ben Zimmer, 'Truthiness', *The New York Times Magazine*, 13 October 2010, https://www.nytimes.com/2010/10/17/magazine/17FOB-onlanguage-t.html (viewed May 2023).

26 Anna Clark, *Making Australian History*, Penguin Random House, Australia, 2022, p. 19.

27 Milan Kundera, 'An Introduction to a Variation', *The New York Times Book Review*, 6 January 1985.

28 Ibid.

29 Timothy Snyder, *On Tyranny: Twenty Lessons from the Twentieth Century*, Crown, New York, 2017, pp. 65–71.

30 Maria Ressa, 'How Social Media Uses Free Speech to Stifle Free Speech', *The Late Show with Stephen Colbert*, YouTube, 30 November 2022, https://www.youtube.com/watch?v=xpWevZ5yQz8 (viewed May 2023).

31 Anthony Horowitz, 'My Clash with Sensitivity Readers', *The Spectator*, 4 February 2023, https://www.spectator.co.uk/writer/anthony-horowitz (viewed May 2023).

32 Mark Mordue, 'Year of the Fool's Skull', *The Slider*, 30 December 2022, https://markmordue.substack.com/p/year-of-the-fools-skull (viewed May 2023).

33 Nicholas Kristof, 'Inclusive or Alienating? The Language Wars Go on', *The New York Times*, 1 February 2023, https://www.nytimes.com/2023/02/01/opinion/inclusive-language-vocabulary.html (viewed May 2023).

34 Saul Bellow, 'The Writer as Moralist', 1963, in Benjamin Taylor (ed.), *There Is Simply Too Much to Think about*, Penguin, New York, 2015.

35 Fyfe, 'Ash, Dylan, Dusty'.

36 Bupa, 'Our Culture', 2023, https://careers.bupa.com.au/our-culture#:~:text=Our%20purpose%2C%20helping%20people%20live,every%20day%20by%20our%20people (viewed May 2023).

37 Christopher Knaus, 'Australia's Biggest Private Health Insurers Illegally Rejected Thousands of Claims', *The Guardian*, 7 July

2019, https://www.theguardian.com/australia-news/2019/jul/08/ australias-biggest-private-health-insurers-illegally-rejected- thousands-of-claims (viewed May 2023).

38 Australian Competition and Consumer Commission, 'Court Orders $6m in Penalties against Bupa and Compensation for Consumers', media release, 12 May 2020, https://www.accc.gov. au/media-release/court-orders-6m-in-penalties-against-bupa- and-compensation-for-consumers (viewed May 2023).

39 Dexter Tilo, 'Bupa CEO "Deeply Sorry" for Underpaying Staff up to $75 Million', *Human Resources Director*, 17 December 2021, https://www.hcamag.com/au/news/general/bupa-ceo-deeply- sorry-for-underpaying-staff-up-to-75-million/320211 (viewed May 2023).

40 Australian Bureau of Statistics, 'Analysis of Non-Binary Sex Responses in the 2021 Census', 27 September 2022, https://www. abs.gov.au/articles/analysis-non-binary-sex-responses (viewed May 2023).

41 Brown, *Dare to Lead*, p. 153.

42 Ibid.

43 The Electric Ben Franklin, 'In His Own Words', https:// www.ushistory.org/franklin/autobiography/page42.htm#: ~:text=Disguise%20it%2C%20struggle%20with%20it,be%20 proud%20of%20my%20humility (viewed May 2023).

44 La Rochefoucauld, *Maxims*, pp. 70–1.

45 Lynn Barber, 'Interview: Look Who's Talking', *The Guardian*, 14 April 2002, https://www.theguardian.com/books/2002/apr/14/ politics (viewed May 2023).

46 Saul Bellow, 'Nobel Lecture', The Nobel Prize, 1976, https://www. nobelprize.org/prizes/literature/1976/bellow/lecture (viewed May 2023).

47 Wolf, *The Crisis of Democratic Capitalism*, p. 7.

48 вареничок.epістaві (@maksymeristavi), *Twitter*, 17 November 2022 (viewed January 2023).

49 Defense of Ukraine (@DefenceU), *Twitter*, 6 January 2023 (viewed January 2023).

50 Mick Ryan, AM (@WarintheFuture), *Twitter*, 8 January 2023 (viewed January 2023).